Prologue

Waggon-time

Last year it seems, yet fifteen years have passed
Since I last felt the waggon lurch and sway
Over the trampled grass towards the Road.
Although for us that world is now long gone,
(We made two roads of it and drove away) . . .
We'll ditch the sense of loss and celebrate –
We struck it rich and lived it for a span;
Hit on a place in time where Gypsy vans
Were still abroad and rolling
That now are only props in neat film fantasies
Or rotting in a *gaujo* garden.

          We were there
To navigate those horsedrawn landships
With their sun-crazed paint and brasswork,
Way-worn galleons of the Travellers' Age of Gold,
Creaking into the troughs and lifting on smooth
      tarmac seas,
Jutting barbarous against the wide sky.

You rode, watchful on the footboard,
The hard ribs of the waggon in your back;
Your arm hooked over the carved bracket beside
      you;
Legs propped on the 'sharps' or swinging
Two feet from the moving road.

You drove, heedful of the changing landscape,
Meeting with mild insolence the stare
Of *gaujos* sealed in prim upholstered cars
(A world away they were and ignorant, you
      thought,
Of all that really counted) . . .

The reins were lapped in your hands and a shaggy
      mare
Pulled steadily as though hypnotised
By the regular beat of her own shod hooves;
the gentle rumble and swing of the waggons,
The click and rattle on the rods
Of worn strap-harness links,
Sometimes a low voice singing
And ahead, the Road.

The Road was your Line-of-Life.
It creaked towards you and slid by
At a steady four-miles-an-hour (so you missed
      nothing)
And though it was not quite
The winding, white road
Edwardian romantics wrote about
(But a kind of dirty grey or brown
And going up and down),
It stretched ahead of you and behind
From horizon to horizon and beyond,
From old friends gone to new aquaintance waiting;
And every story you ever heard or dreamed of
Was just around the corner.

1970

The Gypsies
Waggon-time and After

Denis Harvey

B T BATSFORD LTD · LONDON

To Rita with love

First published 1979
© Denis E Harvey 1979

All rights reserved. No part of this publication may be
reproduced in any form, or by any means, without
permission from the publishers

ISBN 0 7134 1548 7

Set in Monophoto Optima, by
Keyspools Ltd, Golborne, Lancs
Printed by Anchor Press Ltd
Tiptree, Essex
for the publishers B T Batsford Ltd,
4 Fitzhardinge Street, London W1H 0AH

Contents

Preface

Perhaps it is necessary to have lived for a time at least in both worlds, that of the Traveller and that of the housedweller, to begin to appreciate the fact that the two cultures, though fundamentally different, are equally valid. That it is not only perfectly feasible for the two to co-exist, but to do so to their mutual advantage.

It has been the tragedy of the Gypsy people and others of Traveller stock that the attention of the *gaujo* or non-Gypsy has been aroused and often outraged by a class of Traveller who may live a nomadic existence out of poverty, ignorance, or both. Though they too have their moments of grace and grandeur, the fundamental error of confusing the predicament of these deprived outcasts from a sedentary society with the life of travelling people in general has led to much misplaced zeal and inappropriate action on the part of bureaucracy, well-wishers and those with a political axe to grind. The one goal has usually been conversion from the travelling to the sedentary way of life.

In this book my aim has been to preserve some visual record of the best of the travelling life in Britain, as it was and as it is today, in the hope that others besides the Travellers themselves may appreciate something of the qualities of the way of life in this country before it is legislated out of existence.

I was fortunate to stumble on the Gypsy scene at an early age when the big decorated waggons still rolled, the days the Gypsies now call 'Waggon-time', and I began a collection of my own photographs, many of which help to make up this book. For the remaining pictures I

am indebted to others who have trodden or rolled the same road and, where verifiable, these are acknowledged in the text.

The book is dedicated to all Travellers, past, present and, I hope, future.

As far as practicable no personal names of living Travellers appear in the book as this might prove an unwelcome intrusion on their privacy.

Introduction

Travellers in Britain   There is little reason to doubt that there has been an indigenous population of nomads of one kind or another in Britain from prehistoric times. The features of many non-Romani Travellers suggest early origins in Celt and Saxon. The first Romani to enter the country seem to have come by way of Scotland in the 15th century, bearing with them the fictitious tale that they were descendants of the Pharaohs of Ancient Egypt. The word Gypsy, properly spelt with two 'y's, is derived from 'Egyptian'. These 'Gyptians travelled on foot and on horseback in large bands according to tribe and their strangeness engendered fear and suspicion, so much so that in Elizabethan times savagely repressive laws were passed and for many decades just to be a Gypsy was a crime punishable by death. This was not altogether without cause from all accounts for they were a bold people of wild and outlandish appearance and manner, making much use of intimidation and superstition to extract money, food and belongings from the settled population.

Records of their arrival in many countries spreading North and Westward across Europe in the 14th and 15th centuries suggest that they originally came from India. Their speech being a derivation of Sanskrit (now a dead language) further reinforces this supposition. In Britain today the Romany language, *Romanes*, as old Gypsies call it, only survives in a debased form. Nevertheless an astonishing number of Sanskrit words appear to have remained almost intact over perhaps more than a thousand years of wandering, handed on orally down the generations without the help of a written language. It would be strange if the nomadic instinct also – to follow the way of life fostered for a millennium – were not to persist strongly in the Traveller today.

Intermarriage with the settled population used to be extremely rare and was disapproved of by the Gypsy people up to and including the beginning of this century. When such marriages did take place it seems that the *gaujo* or non-Traveller partner was more often than not absorbed into the Travellers' way of life rather than the other way about.

The old saying 'once a Traveller, always a Traveller' holds good even for those today who have 'gone indoors'. In high summer the whole family may go for extended 'holidays' for fruit, potato or pea-picking or to visit horse-fairs and other meetings up and down the country. They still consider themselves to be 'Travelling people'. For most but not all of those who remain on wheels throughout the year, the motor trailer has replaced the living-waggon. Nevertheless the horse, close to the centre of Gypsy culture for so long, still holds an important place in the hearts if not in the economy of many motorised Travellers. Even today at horse-fairs largely supported by travelling people, as many as five hundred horses may change hands. For some Travellers the horse still proves more economically viable than the 'motor', though wayside pitches with sufficient grazing are becoming increasingly few and far between.

Early days

Bender Tents Up till the latter part of the 19th century and the widespread introduction of proprietary-built living-waggons among showmen and itinerant tradesmen, Gypsies commonly travelled with tents, covered carts and pack-animals. Bender-tents date from prehistory. Gypsies in northern latitudes make them from bent ash, hazel or sallow rods covered with blankets, felts or weatherproof sheets. The floor is strewn with carpets and mats and there are raised beds of straw, bracken or fir fronds. Benders come in many sizes and shapes but are usually about 5 feet high, round, half-circle or tunnel-shaped. They have served as homes for Gypsies for at least a thousand years and are far from obsolete even today.

Method of construction The fresh-cut rods, pushed into holes made in the ground with the pointed end of the iron kettle-prop, are bent over and located in adjacent pairs of holes in a ready-made hardwood ridge-pole. This forms a highly efficient frame, firm but resilient, and without the ludicrous inconvenience of guy-ropes and protruding pegs. Covering material is fixed by lapping over and pinning with skewers, fashioned originally of wood toughened by frying in fat, but latterly out of sharpened wire or welding rod.

Left This bender had a headroom of about seven feet and the smoke vent ensured that cooking could be carried on inside in wet weather. The tent could be taken down and packed easily on a donkey or cart (see page 34); only the four or five long poles of the central 'balk' might be jettisoned and cut afresh at each new pitch.

Top right Render Smith and family, c.1910, found a tent of this size quite adequate to house four. A large and well-organised family expecting a lengthy stay could build a bender tent up to 30 feet long, 12 feet wide and 9 feet high, but this was very exceptional (Photo. Fred Shaw)

Bottom right Half-round benders like this one, facing downwind, could be easily added to when weather conditions required it – often by erecting a similar one facing it, to be connected by the smoke vent

Traveller Types

Many brave attempts have been made to classify different categories of Traveller. There are tinkers, mumpers, chorodies, didikais (note 1), pikies, posh-rats (lit. half-bloods), 'full-blooded Gypsies', true Romanies, etc. But these labels are misleading and often carelessly applied; the lines cannot be clearly drawn. Intermarriage between various roughly defined groups, as well as with housedwellers, has made precise classification almost impossible. The black hair and brown eyes of the oriental coupled with the name of one of the early recorded Romani families is some guide to racial origin, but reddish hair and even grey eyes were not unknown in early Romani strains. Certainly, striking similarities still occur between some Gypsy people long-established in Britain and their counterparts in other countries. On the other side of the fence there is no doubt that, as with the Jewish race, Gypsy blood has mingled, often unrecorded, into many areas of *gaujo* society. Bedevilling qualitative identity somewhat further, the self-conscious personality, male or female, is quite capable of emulating in appearance the Romani tradition in varying degrees playing up to the romantic image. Where blood claims are genuine, so be it – there are many who are proud of and wish to reaffirm their origins. There has undoubtedly been a small degree of interrelation between the Gypsies and fairground, circus and canal folk. With a shared interest in horses and a nomadic way of life this is only to be expected, but the amount of overlapping seems to have been minimal; they have always looked on each other as being 'a different class of people'. In

Left Northamptonshire Smiths at the turn of the century

Top right Coopers and Lees on Epsom Downs, Derby-time 1910. Some characteristic Romani faces. *Chavvies* (children) are often fair-haired when young, to go dark or black-haired as they grow older (Photo. Fred Shaw)

Bottom right Smiths, Bucklands, Does, Winmans, Baths – families in some degree interrelated by marriage – are all represented here; part of a large group reunited at fruit-picking time to exchange news and for the young to renew acquaintance with their cousins. They are photographed here in front of an early type of Showmans' living-waggon. Whalebone corsets and ostrich feather hats were much in vogue (*c.* 1908)

Below Smiths again; a closer look at the family with the bender. If they were raised in elegance and wore fine clothes who would detect any Gypsy in them? (1910) (Photo. Fred Shaw)

Top right Bucklands, Smiths, Lees and Boswells; some Romani aristocracy grouped in front of a bender. A *gaujé rawni* (non-Gypsy lady), a friend, poses in tableau with her child while the Gypsy reads her hand

Bottom right Three Gypsies on Walton Downs, Surrey in 1923. In a cloth cap anyone looks English Imagine the young *rom* in a turban (Photo. Fred Shaw)

the last analysis the identity of the Traveller can only be established by family descent and is best recognised through cultural characteristics such as a nomadic tradition, knowledge of the group language, self-employment, manner of speech, style of dress, domestic taste, customs and rituals of cleanliness (note 2) of which more anon.

'Welsh' Woods and Lees at Caernarvon in the 1920s. The Welsh Gypsies have the reputation among English Travellers as being 'real deep Romani'. Many speak *Romanes* in a pure inflected form

Top right Irish Travellers at Yalding, 1948. Finding living easier in England, they have increased in number since the War. Today some very 'flash' Irish Travellers work the country from end to end on the track of antique and secondhand furniture

Bottom right Scottish Travellers stopping on the shores of Loch Eriboll, Sutherland, in 1939. They are twenty miles from the nearest populated region but there are salmon in the Loch; grouse and hare on the 'hill' (Photo. E. Chambré Hardman)

Left South-country Smiths stopping at Corkes Meadow, St. Mary Cray, 1947

Left below These two *Romani foki*, still horsedrawn and happy with it in the 1970s, were stopping with van horse and dogs on the Farnham Bypass in Surrey

Scrap-dealer/horse-dealer and his wife surrounded by their assets in 1977. A magnificent blend of tradition and innovation

Above A group of *juvals*, *raklies* and *chavvies* (women, girls and children) taken at a wedding in 1947

Below The same family at a wedding in 1978. All are now 'indoors' but still independent and proud of their background

The Romani Men

The men, the *mooshes*, the *Roms*, in these pictures hail from different families and different parts of the country but facial characteristics demonstrate that they are strongly linked by the *kaulo ratti*, the dark blood.

One of the Taylors, photographed in 1970, from the North-west but now travelling mostly in S.E. England; still with horses and waggons

Oliver Lee, 'Welsh' Gypsy, photographed 'chinning the cosh' (cutting a stick) at Llangollen in 1913 (Photo. Fred Shaw)

Right Manfred Wood, Traveller, author, and President of the Gypsies' organisation, the Romany Guild

Far right Ithal Lee, Cheshire, 1938

Below right Elder statesman of the Gypsy people, the late Gordon Boswell, whose autobiography was published in 1970 (note 3). Photographed here with one of his sons at Appleby in 1974

The Juvals

It was a hard life, particularly in Waggon-time, to be a woman among Travellers. Apart from the rigours and deprivations accepted as a matter of course, along with the usual woman's role of wife, mother, cook and housekeeper, she often had to tramp many miles in a day 'calling' from door to door with a heavy basket on her arm. The *juvals*, resourceful, tough and resilient, were often handsome as well. The same is true today.

Left A Heron woman leans at the door of her
waggon, c. 1915

Young Smith *juval*, 1910

Left One of the Woods at Lee Gap, Yorkshire, in
1930

Far left Old Darklas Price with Lee grandchildren, Epsom Downs, 1931 (Photo. Fred Shaw)

Left Romani woman at Barnet in the 1940s

Bottom left Womenfolk at Appleby New Fair in 1978

Weather-worn and battle-torn, an old Gypsy *rawni* at Outwood, 1966

The Raklies

The girls help their mothers with domestic chores, take charge of the younger ones, or go 'calling' with the older women. They do not leave the *atchin'-tan* (camp) alone, nor go alone with a boy unless marriage is intended.

Epsom Downs, 1905

Boswells in Derbyshire, c. 1912 (Photo. Fred Shaw)

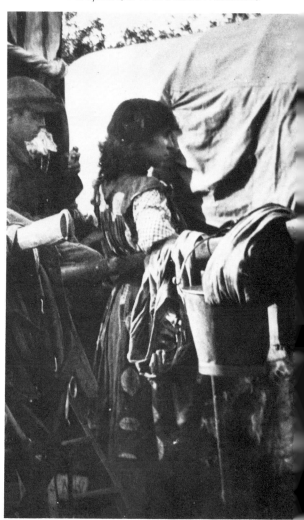

Above Young *raklies* on Gallows Hill, Appleby, 1976

Above Horse-fair, 1974

Below Appleby, Westmorland, 1975

The Chavvies

What Francis Hindes Groome wrote of Gypsy children in the 1870s is as true today. 'Odd compounds of pluck and shyness, of cheek and courtesy, of thoughtlessness and meditation, of quicksilver gaiety and quaint old-fashionedness.' Gordon Boswell, reminiscing in 1970 about his own childhood, said, 'Our lives at that time was continuous happiness and play.' One can make some allowance here for rose-tinted nostalgia, but Gypsy children have ever been indulged and allowed plenty of freedom. Nevertheless they had their routine chores such as *kettering coshties* (collecting firewood), harness-cleaning and water-carrying. Lacking sophisticated toys, their play was closely bound up with nature and animals, and with emulating the work activities of parents and older brothers and sisters. This fostered the spontaneous growth of intelligence and awareness and was sound preparation for the independent livelihood of the roads. Formal education, learning to read and write, has only recently become an important aid to living.

Lee *chavvies* with their father at Epsom, 1931
(Photo. Fred Shaw)

Left Lovell *chavvy*, Derbyshire, 1913

Below left In Dorset, 1973. The muddy boot on the footboard beside him belongs to his father who was standing over him playing the fiddle when the picture was taken

Below Appleby, Westmorland, 1971

The Road

'From horizon to horizon and beyond . . .'

The Road, the *Drom*, the Line-of-Life that makes freedom and independence possible, deserves a capital letter in the Gypsies' book. A horse and waggon, though travelling at only four miles an hour, can effectively vanish in a short time, each fork or turn-off stacking the odds against all but the most relentless pursuit. The experienced eye could follow marks left by iron-shod wheels on the road but road surfaces today do not always reveal these traces and they soon become obliterated by rain or erased by motor-tyres.

The signs left by Gypsies for their own kind are various. They may leave one by the ashes of the fire when pulling off, to show where they are going, who they are, and how many; and also mark the turn-offs on the road with a *patrin* for those coming behind — a tuft of grass pulled from the hedge. More often there is no sign left at all.

Barring interference by police or local authorities there are several factors that may determine when a move should be made. Travelling with horses, grazing is an important consideration and a move may need to be made when the grass gets eaten down. Always there is the necessity to get a living, a change of area from time to time being essential to such activities as dealing, knife-grinding or hawking goods round the houses. Travellers move into specific areas for trade-fairs, horse-fairs and seasonal cropping.

Waggon tracks on the road. Four vans and at least two 'flats' have passed this way since the last rain. Much can be read; for instance, the slower the vehicle the more crooked the line, but it still needs a practised eye

The *patrin*; probably few besides Travellers would notice this sign on the corner, which marks the road the waggon has taken

Distances covered vary considerably, but with horses ten miles in a day is an average shift of range. Fifteen to eighteen miles, with breaks, is as much as most horses can easily pull a big waggon in one day. In warm weather the best time is made in the early morning when the air is cool and the surface of the road is hard. The cushion-effect of a tarred surface on a warm summer day is a considerable drag on a waggon. The unofficial record for horses and waggons is sixty miles on a long winter's night out of Wales, but this was under the pressure of an exceptional emergency.

For communications and fast travel a trap or flat-cart is used. A good horse, well looked after, will keep up a spanking trot for mile upon mile, and in this way important news, passed from one to another, could cross the country from end to end in a surprisingly short time.

Now that Waggon-time is waning and the Trailer Age is here, the Travellers' home can if necessary travel the length of England in an easy day's drive behind a lorry or pick-up. There are advantages and disadvantages in this. A 'Motor' does not fill its own tank overnight the way a horse does and though grazing space is not a requisite for stopping, with the cost of petrol, tax and insurance the increased mobility has not led to much increase in freedom.

Above Welsh Gypsy Matthew Wood poses here (*c.* 1910) with blankets, rods and kettle strapped to a patient moke. Many would have travelled this way in the old days and a few do even today in Ireland and Scotland. The photograph is a little contrived; you pack more than four rods for a bender, and the blankets look as if they have never been used. They may have belonged to the *gaujo* aficionado who took this classic picture

Herons (*left*) and Boswells respectively, parked at the curb in the High Street at Brough about to leave after the Fair in 1911. These sleeping-carts, typical of a Gypsy entourage of the period, supplemented the living-waggons and tents and helped transport provisions and gear (Photo. Fred Shaw)

Four distinct types of horsedrawn van are in this convoy approaching the hop-fields in Horsmonden, Kent, in 1949. Front to rear: Reading, Showman, Ledge, and converted baker's van. The young colt attached on the off-side of the shaft-horse of the leading van gets acquainted this way with motor traffic and the ways of the road. A water jack is slung on the cratch at the rear ready to be filled when passing through a village. Stove-pipes are always on the off-side to avoid argument with roadside trees. The awning fixed to the porch of the second waggon, though once a common accessory, was already a rarity when this picture was taken

Leaving the fair, 1970

Top left and above Two classes of flat-cart, perhaps the most useful vehicle of all. Good for fast travel, they are also used for carrying trade goods, or loading tents and gear for transport between stopping places. With the seat unbolted the whole family can pile on to drive to the pub or into town for a spree. Sometimes these 'spinners' are fitted with a detachable 'accommodation top' for sleeping

Left A cavalcade on the Great North Road near Grantham in 1970; five horses, two loaded trolleys and an Open-lot. These Travellers were on their way north by stages to Yorkshire and Westmorland and would take in the horse-fairs at Appleby and Borough Bridge before moving south again

Left Hazards of the fast road; turning off (Photo. Daniel Harvey)

Traffic-shy horses pull at an erratic trot while heavy lorries roar by like rockets to the moon. In the event natural exuberance can turn potential nightmare into an exhilarating adventure

The ultimate indignity – but much rarer than the films would have you believe: a sprung lynch-pin and a lost wheel. First essential is to straighten the lock and chock the front wheels, as here (if the lock moved round the van would overturn). Then find the pin! This van was moving again within minutes

Above Two classes of horsedrawn van. *Left* the 'old family waggon', newly restored for the Smiths of Doncaster, 'horsing it' to Appleby New Fair in 1978. The 'sider', the horse hitched alongside the one in the shafts, helps with the load – the traces running back to a spreader or swingle-tree attached to the off-side summer. This is common practice on the road with living waggons. *Right* With a more humble, work-a-day turnout, but clearly no less cheerful, these Surrey Travellers were on the move in 1960 (Photo. John Pockett)

All the hallmarks of the successful trade in scrap metal. A lorry with hydraulic grabs carries the family limousine, a Mercedes. The living accommodation in tow is a typical 'Travellers' Special', a Westmorland Star trailer, designed specifically to cater for the tastes of the flash Traveller.

The Stop

The Gypsy going the road, *jalling* the *drom*, is no 'stranger in a hostile land'. On the contrary, he has usually felt himself to be an indigenous entity in a familiar country – albeit a country that has been quite arbitrarily and unfairly colonised by housedwellers, many of whom are suspicious and unfriendly. The *atchin'-tan*, or stopping place, is a haven, and as such is nearly always beautiful. The concept of the 'homeless vagabond' is a *gaujo* one; home is where you light your fire.

Chaw ta pani, grass and water, are the first essentials for a good draw-in for horse-waggons. Grazing problems could sometimes be overcome by passing the horses into a farmer's field, either by arrangement or after dark. Water could be picked up along the road where not refused by housedwellers. It would be carried in water-jacks of tin-lined copper and brass or, more recently, of stainless steel. It was once a common sight to see Gypsies riding their horses to water in a nearby river, stream or pond.

Being moved on by the police became increasingly common with the growth of population and the fencing off of traditional stopping-places by local authorities. Most villages and inhabited localities harbour at least one neurotic or resentful inhabitant capable of phoning the police to keep the Gypsies moving on through. Travellers on a regular circuit who can contain their own resentment at unfair treatment and leave a camp-ground in good order when moving on, are less likely to have trouble of this kind. Unfortunately it is only the untidily left pitch that gets noticed. Critics would do well to reflect that there is hardly a housedweller living who has moved house without leaving some unwanted junk behind. The majority of Travellers seem to care little about rubbish and untidiness outside the van or

'Waiting for the Fair', c. 1905. Lining the roadside Reading, Ledge and Bowtop vans alternate with rod-and-blanket tents, Striped sunsheets in position on the van on the left would be protecting expensive paint decoration and gilded carving.

Right Waiting for the Fair, 1975. The mode of transport has changed; the way of life dies hard or not at all

Left Roadside stop in a grove of hollies around 1900. Location unknown

The traditional *atchin'-tan* on the top of Epsom
Downs near the Racecourse in 1910. Richard
Jefferies wrote of a Gypsy camping place in 1870:
'They have camped here for so many years that it is
impossible to trace when they did not. It is wild still
like themselves. Nor has their nature changed any
more than the nature of the trees.' Compare the
picture with the one in the Introduction which is of
the same spot forty years later

trailer (considered a work area) and this looks like squalor to housedwellers who lean more
heavily than they perhaps realize on the work of the dustmen. Not so often noticed is that the
interiors of the vans are almost invariably kept spotlessly clean.

There are still places in this country where you can pull off the road along an old grass-
grown lane that was never put down to tarmac and there find space to down shafts and
graze the horses out of sight of the jealous eyes of authority. But these places are rapidly
dwindling in number. Many traditional stops, in more or less regular use by travelling people
for hundreds of years past, are being ploughed under or built over. With the coming of heavy
earth-moving machinery and the craze for faster roads, whole landscapes are disrupted and
radically changed in the space of a few days. Many a beautiful stop has vanished forever or
lost all association with its past. The pictures in this section show a fair range of types of
atchin'-tan, from heath and lane-side to suburban wasteland. In the cities many yards owned
or rented by travelling people, usually in areas nobody else wanted, such as beside the
gasworks, served as winter quarters or as transit stops for relatives passing through.

Top A Gypsy stop by the River Mole, 'Little Egypt',
North of Dorking Gap on a summer evening in 1950

Above The same view twenty-eight years later. The
course of the river has been altered and the road is
being re-routed

The night fire – 'a beacon in the dark and friendless
world beyond its light.' Scenes like this, with the
shadows jumping on the waggon-front, the trees
black against the greenish darkening sky – and the
munch and stamp of the horses dragging their
plug-chains over the grass – are perpetually
recorded in every Traveller's heart

Right The pitch in winter. A van can be beautifully
warm within five minutes of lighting the stove;
closing the windows in the mollicroft (skylight), you
can get it hot enough to make a candle wilt. But
when the fire dies down in the small hours of a
frosty winter's night the woodwork twangs with the
cold and your frozen breath sticks blankets to the
wall

Above Conference at Corkes' Pit, 1947. This is 'the Pit' or 'Corkes Meadow' at St. Mary Cray in Kent; an area of suburban wasteland owned by a Traveller which was increasingly resorted to as civic pride and prejudice began to close the traditional stops

Lane-end on Bedford Levels, Cambridgeshire, 1970.
This travelling family, well-known and respected in
those parts, could look out round the horizon and
see twenty-five of their horses grazing in the
evening sunlight

Right Summer and winter roadsides *c.* 1962. *Bottom
right* Laneside stop in Kent (Photo. John Pockett).
Above Travellers on the side of the busy A2 after
eviction from Darenth Woods by the Church
Commissioners

51

When days are getting short: manoeuvring onto a pitch away from view in the October woods. A lad clings to the bow to fend off branches that threaten to knock the stove-pipe

Right The Camp in the Forest, New Style. Two views of a 'Little Egypt' near Thurrock in Essex, 1978. The wind is still on the heath but the trees are made of steel and on a clear day factories line the horizon. Nevertheless this old gravel pit is a beautiful and very welcome haven

A family of Travellers comprising two generations mixing the old and the new way of life in 1978. In the foreground, an Open-lot living-van and a Dunton waggon. Behind them were three flat-carts and a lorry and trailer with a pile of scrap just being off-loaded for sorting; another Open-lot beyond.

The camp was alive with game fowls running loose, two or three long-dogs and the drifting smoke from three stick fires. At least ten horses cropped the wild meadow grass in the middle distance. A more pleasant or healthier sight it would be hard to imagine

The Horse

The horse, the *grai*, at the centre of Gypsy culture for so long, appears in facsimile on waggons, carts and lorries alike, as well as in effigy inside the trailers, as an emblem of the travelling life. Horse-dealing has long been either a sideline or a major occupation for many travelling people in Britain. In the old days a regular trade could be looked for from farmers and other private individuals, coaching and freighting businesses, the coal pits and the Army. There was a steady run-down of demand for horses in the twenties and thirties but, since the war, trade has picked up considerably. Although some horses on offer at horse-fairs and sales may end up as tinned meat and hides, the better ones find their niche for breeding purposes, for pulling trolleys, for hunting, racing, riding-schools and private hacking and driving. There is still a fair living to be had with horses for the travelling man with generations of experience behind him, who can carry out veterinary treatment that may be necessary or desirable, and do his own shoeing – both potentially costly items.

Many Travellers who have long gone over to motor transport retain an active interest in horses and where trailers are pulled in along the roadsides it is a common sight to see a coloured horse or two (skewbald or piebald) or a child's pony. These would travel in a covered lorry, van or horse-box. It is largely due to the Traveller's predilection for a coloured horse that the percentage of piebald and skewbald horses has increased enormously over the last few decades.

Back in Waggon-time, for pulling a living-waggon carrying women and children, a strong, quiet and experienced van-horse was essential. Such horses were not to be sold under any normal circumstances and became solid and respected members of the family. Hazards on the road are many. A horse not used to Gypsy vans can be panicked by the unaccustomed high overhang of the waggon-porch and many a disastrous runaway has resulted from this alone. Along with that risk, a horse uninitiated to waggon life may be disconcerted by the apparent size of the load, having no way of understanding that a Gypsy

A spotted'n; a triumph of breeding by a motorised Traveller who has not lost interest in horses (Photo. Daniel Harvey)

A fair-sized vanner, about 15.2 hh (15½ hands) high, being hitched in to a 'Square bow' living-van. Cross-shire, with a touch of Clydesdale? Lineage is often hard to trace. The elaborate harness, much coveted by Travellers, carries white-metal buckles, clips and keepers, and rams-horn hames. Carriage-lamps, though shown here, were not commonly displayed. Towards the end of the day, to have no lights was an insurance against being moved on.

Sturdy cobs of about 14 hh suitable for pulling an open-lot van.

van is hollow. Again, if a disheartened or stubborn horse stops and then jibs (goes into reverse) on a steep hill, a serious accident can rapidly result. Retaining a mare rather than a gelding for the responsible role of shaft-horse enabled the owner to breed from her and this was common practice.

The Dogs

The dog, the *jukel*, is a vitally important part of the Gypsy ménage. Not only can a good one be relied upon to stock the pot with hares and rabbits, but it is also an essential for guarding the waggon, tent or trailer. Although good waggon-dogs come in all shapes and sizes and a 'likely one' like Harry Wood's (right) is popular, the Lurcher is probably the favourite Gypsy breed. A typical Lurcher is a cross between Greyhound and Collie, Deerhound, Wolfhound, Bedlington, Alsation, Doberman or Poodle. It is bred to combine the speed of the greyhound with the character and intelligence of the cross-breed. The name Lurcher is thought to derive from the ability when coursing a hare to anticipate the dodging of the quarry and turn with it, where a Greyhound tends to overshoot and lose much ground. It is a characteristic of a Lurcher that, though a fearsome and formidable antagonist to an intruder, it is often an exceptionally gentle, friendly and reliable dog within the family circle. A good dog would be trained to catch or retrieve game and carry it straight to the waggons, and some to locate hedgehogs for the pot.

Below Lurcher: Greyhound and Scottish Deerhound cross

Top left Portrait of Harry (Turpin) Wood with *jukel*

Top right Lurcher: Greyhound and Welsh Collie cross

Right An old long-dog at home in Fenland

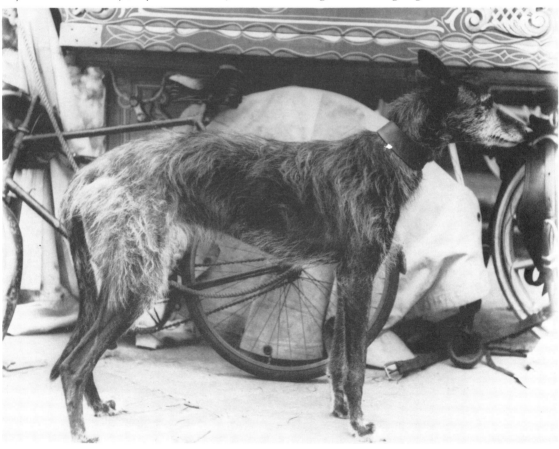

58

Growing Up with Animals

Travellers' children are brought up in the knowledge and understanding of animals. Dogs and horses are often treated and loved like members of the family. Living amongst the hedgerows, heaths and woods the children were surrounded by animals and birds of many kinds. Pets included foals, puppies, goats, chickens and bantams, baby rabbits, fledgeling game birds and even crows and magpies from the wood.

Travellers' Fashion

The pictures here, not being specifically photographs of dress, cannot be fully comprehensive. They serve as an indication only, but are for the most part typical of a culture that has over the past one hundred years maintained a distinctive style of its own, even today retaining strong links with its own fashion of earlier years. Gypsies have ever admired 'a bit of Old-faash'nd'; the words 'old-fashioned' being commonly used as a term of approbation. Although much of their style seems to derive from Victorian England there are strong elements that appear unique, such as the elaborately stitched and pleated aprons worn by the women and the distinctive cut and quadruple rows of stitching on the men's suits. There were tailors and factories around the country who catered for the Travellers' special tastes in clothing, hats and footwear (note 4).

The Men   Coats for the men were of heavy cloth, dark brown or green, cut with a yoke and sometimes a back-belt. They carried five double-stitched patch pockets with button-down flaps bordered with four rows of stitching. Inside was a breast pocket and a deep poacher's pocket capable of hiding hare, pheasant or a 'parcel of trout'. Buttons would be of horn

A quadruple-stitched coat worn here with the high-waisted, drop-fronted trousers, soft black velour hat and a flash silk *diklo*. The wife wears an embroidered and scalloped 'pinna' in black silk

Far left A picture strongly redolent of domestic style and taste in the hey-day of Waggon-time. A daughter of Bui Boswell and Saviana Lovell with two of her children on the steps of a Tong waggon similar to that described by Gypsy Sylvester Gordon Boswell in his recent autobiography (note 3). The clothes, the boots, the lace, the waggon carving, the patterned frosted glass and the rag rug are all typical of English Gypsy domestic accoutrements and décor at the turn of the century.

Right Tom and Comfort Stevens at Herton, Bucks, 1924. Paisely shawl; five-pocketed suit (Photo. Fred Shaw)

sometimes trimmed with silver.

Trousers, of corduroy, 'moleskin' or other heavy cloth were cut very high and had a drop-fronted fly with seven rows of stitching round the flap. They were double-seated, very roomy, but tailored fairly close to the knee for riding horseback. Turnups would have five rows of stitches and sometimes spade-shaped 'kick-patches' on the inside bottom edge.

Many travellers of course had to settle for cast-offs from housedwellers when a sporty, racy, horsey cut or otherwise flamboyant style was favoured.

The favourite *stardi* (hat) was a trilby of soft black velour worn without the dent. Gypsy youths liked to wear a 'Fred Sloan' cap with a long squarish peak, named after the famous jockey (see p. 28). A coach whip or the old waggoners' whip banded with brass down the length of the stock was an important accessory of the dressed-up travelling man.

Neckerchiefs (*diklos*) were of yellow or patterned silk and are favoured to this day, though not often for everyday wear now since it can prejudice business contacts with the *gauji*.

Belts, when worn, would be in conjuction with braces. A characteristic design had twin horsehoe buckles in white-metal or nickel connecting a central front strap, the arrangement a miniature version of a girth strap. The centre piece, as with harness, might be ornamented with white-metal mountings.

Hair   Glossy black ringlets of the Victorian Gypsy gave way to the fringe style for the front locks or the curled forelock of the country labourer, whilst quite often young men and boys had their hair close-cropped. From the Fifties and well into the 1970s most young travelling men favoured the early 'Elvis Presley' cut. Travellers' fashion today shows a similar trend of

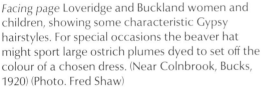

Facing page Loveridge and Buckland women and children, showing some characteristic Gypsy hairstyles. For special occasions the beaver hat might sport large ostrich plumes dyed to set off the colour of a chosen dress. (Near Colnbrook, Bucks, 1920) (Photo. Fred Shaw)

Above A Boswell *rakli* in white silk dress with puff sleeves and lambskin shawl, silk *diklo*, high-laced boots and stays. Her father has a deep-pocketed tail coat typical of everyday wear

Above right Talaitha Cooper in Paisley shawl and crocheted Gypsy apron, with her daughter Polly – one-time familiar figures at Epsom Races (Photo. Fred Shaw)

Right Dressed for 'calling'; showing the method of coping with a heavy child and a hawking basket while having your hands free for *dukkerin'* (fortune-telling) and counting the change (Photo. Frank Cuttriss) (note 5)

A handsome Burton woman leans on the shaft of a waggon wearing characteristic pleated and embroidered apron, amber beads, and cross-over scarf fastened with a golden crown brooch (Photo. Edward Harvey)

Right Young Gypsy women of the late Forties

Far right Typical Travellers' hairstyle of the Fifties, or any time (Photo. Tony Boxall)

following current hairstyles but the ultra-long hair of the 'hippie' is shunned.

In the late Forties men tended towards 'spiv'-style suits with padded shoulders, baggy trousers, silk ties and snap-brimmed hats reminiscent of the American Thirties, worn with pointed brown and white shoes of scalloped and punch-patterned leather. Today expensive pin-striped suits are still worn, with waistcoats and red, blue or patterned fashion shirts; for utility wear, fisherman's-knit cardigans with leather buttons. Trousers, normally supported by braces, are worn short enough in the leg to reveal elastic-sided dealers' boots in orange or yellow leather – the cult of the Horse reasserting itself.

The Women   A Scotch plaid has throughout the last one hundred years perhaps been the most favoured material worn by Gypsy women, still appearing on special days and at horse-fairs around the country. At the turn of the century dresses with tight bodices, long full skirts and sleeves puffed to the elbow might be made of plaid, plush or silk, trimmed with lace or velvet. For older women black satin was often chosen. Younger women and girls might have Summer dresses of grey-, blue- or red-and-white check gingham (see pages 28 and 71). The commonest wear was a blouse and tight-waisted skirt to just above the ankles, a pleated apron with broad-fronted waist band, and high buttoned or laced boots with $2\frac{1}{2}$ inch heels. This apron (*jodaka*), worn not for domestic purposes but when out and about, was an important and smart article of dress. On the finest the two deep side-pockets were embroidered with flower patterns in coloured thread and finished with point-patterned edges and five rows of stitching. They were made from a shiny, satin-smooth black cloth imported from Italy.

Silk scarves or wrap-around shawls were fastened with a brooch and often worn with beads of amber and coral. Silk squares or triangles were used to cover the head and either tied below the chin or knotted in turban style behind the head. Some women would wear a broad leather belt with a massive metal buckle and this could serve as a formidable weapon in time of need.

Underclothes were of red flannel or white calico, petticoats for special occasions being full, frilly and embroidered. One or two underskirts were also worn. It was common practice in winter to wear for everyday use several layers of clothing, or several dresses, under a wrap-around 'pinna'. The abundance of washing at the average Gypsy camp bore testimony to this

Facing page Bridesmaid's
dress and contemporary
interior décor.
(Antimacassars are out –
transparent polythene
in).

Far right A characteristic
emerging today is the
profusion of richly
contrasting colours,
patterns and textures.

practice until fairly recently. Immediately beneath the 'pinna' the Gypsy wife commonly wore a deep canvas *putsi* or pocket slung from her waist (see page 8), in the old days taking charge of the family cash.

In the Thirties, Forties and Fifties it was common to see little *raklies* wearing long or three-quarter-length dresses, in contrast to the short, high-waisted frocks of *gaujo* children of the same age. Such dresses for everyday wear could be readily adapted from the cast-offs from older *gaujo* girls, begged whilst out calling or salvaged from rag-collection from the houses of the rich. Party dresses were particularly common; the well-to-do housedwellers did not care for the same dress to be worn too often, so there was a liberal turnover.

Hair-styles   Women's hair was almost invariably plaited or braided but with any number of ingenious variations on the theme, using coloured ribbons, decorative clips and slides, or side-combs of tortoise-shell, silver-mounted or set with imitation diamonds. Hair was washed, dried and treated with mutton-fat or butter – rubbed in and well brushed out – or combed with soapy water to make it shine. This practice has now been widely abandoned for more sophisticated treatment but you might still see an old Romani woman with soap-

stiffened locks raking forward like ram's-horns over her brown and wrinkled cheeks.

Jewellery was, and remains, heavy gold or silver, much sought after or handed down as family heirlooms. Massive rings worn by both men and women are in the form of strap-and-buckle, gold sovereign, snake, or inter-woven turk's-head plait. Brooches for fastening shawl or scarf are made from commemorative crown pieces, arrangements of half-sovereigns, or of heavy silver inset with coloured stones. Also of recurring popularity are beads of heavy amber, or several strings of red coral. Earrings were again made from sovereigns or half-sovereigns but are more often variations on the drop or the crescent. The little *raklies*, perhaps from the age of seven or eight, sport small plain gold rings or crescents in their ears.

In many areas since the war it was found that to dress in noticeably Traveller-fashion could prejudice trade, but this applied to the men rather than the women. I have in mind a group of Cooper and Smith womenfolk setting off one bright morning in the late Fifties from Effingham Common where they were stopping. They were wearing 'pinnas' of white satin with bright tartan skirts showing below to just above the ankles; at their necks silk *diklos* of orange and green which set off their copper-brown faces and glossy hair; in their ears heavy crescent or drop earrings of embossed gold. Each carried on her arm a large loop-sided hawking basket lined with Brussels lace, loaded with batches of freshly cut clothes-pegs of clean white hazel and bright tin. They took the train to Worcester Park, to go calling in the suburban streets of Southwest London. A more attractive group of people you could not wish to trade with.

Cooking Arrangements

Although living-waggons contained cast iron cook stoves similar to the galley stoves in small ships, cooking was, and often still is, mostly done on a 'stick fire' outside with pot, kettle and frying-pan or skillet hung from kettle-props; a speedy, efficient and economical way of cooking for those who are familiar with it. Even in Britain the weather is seldom so bad as to make cooking outdoors impracticable. In the old days to avoid damage to turf in inhabited localities, fires would sometimes be built in large three-legged iron dishpans. This practice has died out, perhaps because in more recent times Travellers were rarely permitted to camp close to any centre of habitation. Today a stick-fire for cooking is commonly made on the ground, the operational part of the fire covering an area about two feet in diameter.

Most useful cooking pots are the two- and four-gallon oval boilers made in the old days in cast iron, now in pressed steel, and tinned on the inside; a cast iron frying pan (made in three sizes) with pouring lip and overhead handle fitted with a swivel-ring for hanging from the kettle-prop; and an eight- or sixteen-pint kettle, again in cast iron and tin-lined.

Outside fires need protection from the wind to ensure a steady heat and a 'lue' screen would sometimes be erected from a sheet fixed on rods to windward. The cooking of different items of food could be carried out in the same large pot, tied up in separate cloth bags, either dropped in the pot or hooked over the rim. Roasting in the old days might be on a spit

Left A forest of kettle props. *Cordon noir* cooking to the uninitiated but a most efficient and economical method for those familiar with it

Top right A chittie (tripod) could safely support a heavier pot than a kettle-iron but the use of it seems to have declined considerably around the turn of the century

Top left The 'Hostess', the most popular waggon stove from c. 1895, was made of cast iron with a brass guard rail and a brass-fronted coal box that fitted like a drawer underneath. There was a small oven and two hot-plates. Six and eight-pint kettles, copper or plated, were designed with a 'well bottom' that recessed down onto the hot coals when a top plate was removed

Above O'Neills, Travellers of Irish descent for some time resident in England, incorporate hedge and ralli-cart as support for a lue-sheet to windward. The family china is out and tea is in progress. The Ledge waggon, built by Tom Tong of Bolton, is one of the finest examples of the type. c. 1916

attached to a metal tray or in a Dutch oven – a large iron boiler with a heavy lid containing a whistling steam vent. This was banked up in the hot embers of a large fire.

Meals   Breakfast is normally a fry-up such as bacon or – but only recently – processed meat, eaten between thick slices of white bread, or the bread too might be fried in the pan. In the usual Travellers' day the next meal, the main one, will not be prepared till around half past four, or when the more routine side of making a living is over for the day and the women are back from calling. Tea is the favourite beverage, liberally dispensed at any time of day, with or without evaporated milk, and with plenty of sugar.

With perhaps two notable exceptions Gypsy food is much like any other, though with the more regular inclusion in past times of rabbit, hare, trout and pheasant. Details of mode of capture of these is beyond the scope of this book, except to mention that the one that has perhaps gathered the most mystique, but in practice requires the least skill, is 'tickling' trout.

Food peculiar to Gypsies in this country is the much-renowned hedgehog (*hotchiwichi*), and snails (*bauri*). Bread is a staple food. 'Travellers of all classes have a respect for their bread that is almost Biblical', writes Brian Raywid (note 6) '... a society that respects its bread has retained the memory of lean times and is ever reminded that they can return.' Bread is eaten with all food, occasionally with jam, but rarely with butter or margarine. Tinned food has become acceptable to Gypsy people only comparatively recently, having been viewed with distaste long after it became standard fare amongst the *gauji*.

China   used for eating and drinking is of good quality and any cracked or chipped item was and still is destroyed forthwith, as it becomes *mockadi*. The term sounds like slang (muckety) but the word is *Romanes* and has its root in Sanskrit; it is used in the sense of 'unclean' rather than merely dirty. It is also *mockadi* to wash yourself or your clothes in the same bowl that is used for washing the vegetables or the food utensils, each operation having a separate bowl assigned to it. Those who do not observe this code are considered to be 'dirty people'.

Left *Hotchiwichis* are not baked in clay as the *gaujos* will have it. The spines are shaved off, the remaining hair singed; they are then opened out, cleaned and put to soak in salt water, later to be roasted on a spit or stewed

Top Lees at Appleby, 1977. Two and four-gallon cooking pots contain food for perhaps three generations of the family. The *chai* (young woman) holds a stainless steel bowl kept for washing the vegetables

Above A *puri dai* (mother) places puddings, tied up in cloth, into the boiler to simmer

Livelihood

Independence and versatility are the characteristic and essential attributes of the Gypsy. His ability to make some sort of a living wherever he may find himself, whilst remaining his own master, is well demonstrated. This faculty seems to stem, today as much as ever, from a flair for seeing and exploiting the discrepancies in demand and supply of goods, services and seasonal labour at any time and place. Of the essence is the ability to move without fuss or disruption from one area to another as demand arises and is satisfied.

Up till the twilight of Waggon-time craft manufacture – clothespegs, baskets, artificial flowers etc. – and fortune-telling, would supply a steady supplementary income, whilst knife-grinding, dealing in horses and other domestic stock, selling carpets, wicker and cane articles, cheap pottery (seconds), brushes, combs, lace and many other commodities, bulk-bought, could yield a fair living; reinforced as might be by provender from wood, hedgerow, field and stream. For the few, a booth or coconut-sheet on the fairground afforded a reasonable livelihood. Hop, fruit, pea picking and hoeing and other work dependent on a mobile labour force provided pleasant and profitable work in season.

It is ironical that the Gypsy is often accused of laziness and irresponsibility when in fact he shoulders more responsibility than most housedwellers. Dominic Reeve, a highly literate Traveller, pointed out in 1958 (note 7): 'The very essentials of living – wooding, water-fetching, harness maintenance, waggon-repairs, looking after the horses – demand an enormous lot of time . . . these chores are secondary to the actual business of travelling about and endeavouring at the same time to earn sufficient money to keep alive.'

Gypsies, in common with the small farmer, do not have holidays. 'Yer 'olidays' is a *gaujo* phenomenon and related in the Gypsies' mind with the wage-slave. The word might be used by Travellers (especially those gone indoors) when referring to fruit-picking, or by some as a euphemism for a term in prison.

Levi Carey making rush baskets at a midday laneside stop near Sevenoaks, Kent, c. 1910. The makings of a bender tent are neatly stowed on the spring-cart

Left Peg-cutting at a laneside stop. 1949, near Dorking, Surrey

Right 'Mouthing' the pegs

Bee skeps from dried grass with bramble-stem binding

Flowers from elderwood (Photo. T. Boxall)

Fortune-telling (*dukkerin'*) is still a lucrative business and regular stands at fairground, horse-fair, racecourse or rally are as common as ever. A palm-reading Gypsy out calling can soon detect in conversation if the householder is a likely customer for the service. The late Dora Yates, renowned Gypsiologist and long-time Secretary of the Gypsy Lore Society, records phrases of the dukkering Gypsy woman so characteristic that they deserve to be quoted in full. She writes in her autobiography (note 8) 'I knew all the catchwords, beginning with the impressive: 'You've got no common hand, girl,' or 'There's luck in your lovely face, Lady,' or 'You'll call to rememberment all your life long what the poor Gypsy girl tells you this day,' and the convincing quick interpolations: 'You hunderstands what I mean my Rawnie?' or 'I'm telling you the God's truth, ain't I now?' ...

The old saying 'every Gypsy woman is a witch' is still half-believed by many and the skill of the Gypsy at detecting the kind of person you are, and consequently the kind of experiences you have had, and are likely to have, is sometimes as impressive as Sherlock Holmes's most startling observations. Undeniably intuition – the subconcious – occasionally lends a hand in dukkering, and there have been instances of what seems to be genuine clairvoyance, but such cases are rare.

Crafts Shopping baskets were woven entire, from willow withies or from paper-thin strips of split hazel, on a rigid bent-wood framework. Bee skeps and large lidded baskets for the home were made, coil-structure, from rush, grass or straw bound with bramble stems. For peg-cutting, hazel or willow again was used, with bonding strips cut from food cans and usually fastened with cobblers' gimps. A good peg-maker could turn out a gross of pegs in

One of the traditional jobs of the Gypsy wife is calling from door to door with a basket on her arm loaded with pegs, whittled flowers, brushes, combs, lace and other small household items. When the basket is empty the cash in hand is used to stock it with provisions for the evening and next day. (Dorset c. 1900 or later)

Below Bunching 'daffies', c. 1912 (Photo. Frank Cuttriss)

an hour-and-a-half and sometimes the whole family was employed, each person taking on a different stage of the process, working on the technique of the assembly line. Peg-making along with many other crafts has fallen off greatly, particularly in the Midlands and South-east. In the North and West it is still found a viable proposition. Gypsy pegs are still in important ways superior to the machine-made tweezer-type peg. They do not suffer so readily from mildew and their grip is variable – they can be pressed home more firmly to secure materials on a windy day.

Artificial flowers – chrysanthemum heads whittled from elder sticks, and pink and white roses skilfully fashioned from stretched crepe paper – are mounted on sprays of privet. Good ones have a freshness and vitality that rivals plastic replicas.

Some Travellers had their own craft specialities, such as whips from dyed and plaited rushes or coloured raffia; whittled crosses in bottles – a devout variation on the ship-in-bottle idea; and rustic flower baskets built from thin hazel sticks with a high looped handle, sold complete with flowering primrose plant bedded in moss. Little bouquets of 'daffies', primroses, cowslips, violets and snowdrops were also made up and sold in season.

Dealing in horses, vehicles and almost any other commodity is an essential part of Travellers' craft. Though pride of ownership is as common among Travellers as among the *gauji*, possessiveness is not a characteristic and they rarely own anything that is not negotiable at the right price. The technique of dealing is learnt at an early age. Some are more subtle practitioners of the craft than others. One of the Kentish Smiths was nicknamed Cheapfair because of his monotonous repetition of the two words when pushing a deal. Protestations of honesty are often overdone: 'That's the trufe, I tell'; 'That's *very* true that is'; 'That's as true as *anyfing I ever said*'; 'You wont never 'ear nuffing truer nor that, not if you live to be thousand'. Singularly reliable is: 'On my child's life – on me dear little chavvie's sweet life that's the God's honest trufe that fing what I tell you.'

Left Another lucrative outcome from calling, besides fortune-telling, might be the location of scrap-metal, and tarmacking jobs for the menfolk

Above *Dukkering*, only sometimes done with a crystal ball and then often at extra charge. Palm-reading is the norm and a greater rapport with the client can be established by touch. Epsom Downs, 1927

At the race-course, on the beach, at fairs and Midland 'feasts' a booth like this would be set up – the absolute uniqueness of the fortune-teller always proclaimed. *c.* 1935. The sign below simply says: 'She's good'

Above Some Travellers had their living-waggons fitted with a high roof-rail for carrying wicker chairs, carpets and other goods for trade.

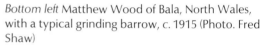

Bottom left Matthew Wood of Bala, North Wales, with a typical grinding barrow, c. 1915 (Photo. Fred Shaw)

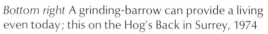

Bottom right A grinding-barrow can provide a living even today; this on the Hog's Back in Surrey, 1974

Horse-dealing requires a lot of knowledge and skill; a profitable sideline for many Travellers, it was, and still is, a major source of income for a few (see above – 'The Horse'). One Traveller, well-known in East Anglia, not unusually has around fifteen to twenty-five horses 'on the hoof'. He recently totalled up ninety-seven and was resisting his daughter's entreaties to get three more and make a century. 'They'd say I was boasting wouldn't they?'

Seasonal cropping Apples, plums, damsons, gooseberries, strawberries, cherries, blackcurrants, hops, peas, potatoes – all could provide work from June through to October. It was heartening for the Gypsy to find he was actually looked for and welcomed by local farmers at such a time. This work is the closest the Traveller ever comes to wage labour – temporary work on a piece-rate basis. Often the entire family, perhaps three or four generations, worked together, though not necessarily as a single wage-earning unit. Life in the hop-fields was unique. Growers would cater for many important needs of the pickers. Along with the piece-work went free-grazing, huts for the towndwellers or for Travellers without tents or vans, sheaves of clean straw to make beds, stand-pipes for water, faggots for fires, fresh milk, eggs and even medical attention might be laid on. September-time could be idyllic. Apples, hops and potatoes are now almost always gathered by machine, but strawberries, plums, gooseberries and peas still require human judgement and manual dexterity in the picking.

Scrap-collecting Although recycling of waste metals is an important economy there is little official provision for collecting and sorting. The bulk of this work is carried out by travelling people some of whom own or rent their own scrap-yards. Both men and women may be

'Haven't you any ambition?' was a question put by an interviewer on a recent T.V. film about a Gypsy horse-dealer's life – possibly because the Gypsy had few material possessions besides a light waggon. Coverage by film, radio and the written word often underrates and belittles such men as these, brilliant in their own field, inarticulate only outside their own circle

A Romani horse-dealer, still living in the old life-style, moves pitch with some of his current stock. Norfolk, 1967

employed collecting and sorting. Aluminium and copper are particularly valuable, but brass, lead, pewter, cast-iron, heavy steel and even light iron sheet are practical propositions. Minimum requirement is a knowledge of metals, a lorry, pick-up or trolley for collecting around houses and works, a sledge-hammer and cutting tools. Most useful is a heavy lorry fitted with a crane, winch or hydraulic grab (see the photo on p. 42).

Rags and Woollens   Door to door collection of cast-offs, and the left overs from jumble sales provide another viable source of income.

Tarmacking   Laying tarmac driveways for private houses and small firms is to some degree simpler than dealing in scrap and rags in that less space is needed. Hot tarmac, bought in the morning, is laid the same day.

Trade in secondhand furniture and antiques, tree-lopping, contract gardening, mowing, dung-selling, roofing, logging and many other activities all add to the list. For Travellers without a yard few of these sources of income are sufficient by themselves. The essence of Travellers' craft is the ability to switch from one to another to meet the need. Establishing their own routes they endeavour not to poach on each others' preserves. Encroachments lead to a lot of 'shout' but such confrontations rarely reach the point where physical violence becomes the only solution.

Waggon-building and restoration   Although Travellers have in the past often improvised their own waggons by building onto or adapting existing vehicles, it is only since the old proprietary builders have finished that those with sufficient skill, and access to working space, have taken up restoring and redecorating waggons on a commercial basis. An Open-

Dealing: Sometimes a quiet and serious affair but often carried out with a great deal of banter, blarney, humbug and high rhetoric. The deal is made and ratified by a slap of the outstretched palm, and this action carries as much weight as the signature on a contract

lot van built on an existing dray, flashed up and lined out, can fetch a lot of money in the right quarter (see 'The Waggons').

Left above Fruit-pickers at Sarisbury, Hampshire, 1905

Left below Eight o'clock in the morning: hop-pickers in Kent, September 1949. On the left are the huts for Londoners or Travellers who came from afar without their tents or waggons. Just visible beyond the waggons is a 'cottage' tent, much liked by the Traveller; six to ten feet square, it contains stove, furniture, and carpets on the floor

Finishing off a neglected strip. Manual dexterity pays high dividends and is acquired early

Above A Londonside Traveller's calling card. This could save both caller and housedweller a lot of time as all knew where they stood; c. 1950

Top Weighing-in

Left Wisbech, 1978. Strawberry picking in East Anglia attracts travellers from as far away as Scotland. It is as near as Gypsies get to the *gaujo* concept of a holiday

Above Sorting the product of a morning's calling for scrap metal, rags and woollens. Copper and aluminium from a washing-machine and lead from car batteries. The girl works alongside her man

The Waggons

In Hungary and Spain the Gypsies are renowned for what they have done with the folk-music of the host country, bringing to it, as they did, their own characteristic qualities of emotional intensity and panache. In Britain it was the caravan that the Gypsies adopted and made peculiarly their own. So much so that it came to be considered almost the symbol of the Gypsy way of life in this country. The travelling showmen who actually pioneered the living-waggon are seldom given credit for having done so. Nevertheless the so-called Gypsy caravan is a peculiarly English product, its counterpart on the Continent of Europe being commonly of far less elegant and specialised design.

The subject has engendered an extraordinary amount of mystique and misconception, often encouraged by the Gypsy himself who will always oblige the inquisitive *gaujo* by telling him what he wishes to hear. Assertions that a van is 'a hundred years old', and decorated with the colours and secret symbols of the tribe, are typical.

The living-waggon was evolved for showmen little more than a hundred and twenty years ago and vans of more than half that age are rare. Constructed mainly of softwood for lightness, few vans survive more than fifty years of English weather and the hard treatment inevitably sustained pulling off the road over rough heathland, hill track and roadside verge.

The Five Types By 1900 the horsedrawn living-waggon had evolved into five distinct types

A superb Reading type van – this one built by Orton and Son of Burton-on-Trent; an old and faded photograph but full of significant period detail. The sun-sheets on the second van were made of a light cotton duck and were hung to protect not only the paint decoration, but the structure itself, from shrinkage – hot sun being a van's worst enemy

Left Sam Dunton of Reading at one time led the field in the manufacture of this type of waggon for Gypsies, and it became known as the 'Reading' shape

of more or less standardised design: the Reading, the Ledge, the Bow-top, the Showman, and the Brush waggon. Of these the first three were preferred by Gypsies. They had tall wheels with a narrowed body slung between – high under-body clearance coupled with a low centre of gravity giving stability over rough terrain. The showmen, accustomed to the more level pitch of fairground and circus tober, tended to prefer the wider floor-space provided by the Showman van which was built out over smaller wheels. The Brush waggon was designed specifically for those who made a living as brush, basket and carpet salesmen.

Few if any of the Brush waggons have survived in original functional form, and of the other types – apart from the few that have been preserved under cover in museums or elsewhere by those with some understanding of timber preservation – most have rotted away or deteriorated beyond the point of no return. Many have been ritually burned on the death of their Gypsy owners.

In addition to the proprietary types listed above, in the Thirties a sixth type evolved, the Open-lot, which is still being built and decorated by Gypsies themselves and is a worthy successor to its now almost extinct forerunners.

All of these caravan types are clearly distinguishable and were evolved to meet a

A ledge waggon by Tom Tong of Bolton, another famous builder – photographed at Brough, Westmorland with some of the Heron tribe in 1911. (Photo. Fred Shaw)

Bow-top by William Wright nearing completion in his yard near Leeds; some gold-leaf is still to be applied to the door panel. Bill Wright's Bow-tops became the type of van most favoured by horsedrawn travelling people, other than showmen, due to its functional elegance, easy maintenance, and under-body clearance combined with a low centre of gravity. The bow was insulated beneath the canvas with pile carpeting or patterned felt. The Wrights drew customers from all over the country including Wales, Scotland and Ireland. (Photo. Albert Wright c. 1905)

ill Wright was also renowned for his two- and four-
wheeled potters' carts, so-called because, fitted
with a canvas tilt, they were used for hawking
seconds from the Potteries around the country.
They were also used as sleeping-carts or
'accommodations' by Gypsies

Detail of the elaborate structure of a Wright pot-
waggon – seen here less shafts and tilt

92

specific need. The original five were nearly always built to order by firms that manufactured trade vehicles of many kinds, not by firms that made vehicles for 'the Gentry'. There were also many home-made vans, 'peg-knife waggons', built on existing underworks by Travellers who could not afford a professionally-built job. Occasionally these emulated the design characteristics of the proprietary types but more often were shaped up according to necessity, using whatever materials were to hand.

General Specification   The typical Gypsy living-waggon is one-roomed on four high wheels with door, shafts and movable steps in front, sash-type windows at the sides and back, and a rack at the back for carrying tents and other gear. Underneath between the rear wheels is the kettle-box for stowing the sooty cooking utensils used on the outside fire. Body measurement being about 10 feet by 6 feet, the whole is capable of being pulled by one horse.

Inside, the built-in furniture and equipment comprises the following: on the left as you enter is a wardrobe cupboard with a small boot or brush cupboard below, a boxed-in fireplace with miniature cast iron cooking range, above it a mirrored overmantel, and a locker-seat under the offside window. On the right or nearside is a glazed bow-fronted

Top left A first class 'Showman' by Orton and Son. The wheels running under gave it more floor-space but less stability – a type best suited to good roads and level tobers

Bottom left A fine Brush waggon, well stocked with its wares. This was the only type of living-waggon that had its door, and steps (fixed ones) at the rear

Now that the old waggon-builders have long since 'finished and gone away' some Travellers have taken to building Open-lots like this one, replacing the old waggons as they fell apart. Fitted with a Hostess or Queen stove these open-fronted vans are warm even in the coldest weather. The front can be closed against wind and rain with shaped canvas curtains hooked round inside the porch

Above Typical little workaday Open-lot with front covers tied back to the bow; no relation to the hardboard and angle-iron travesties recently contrived by firms offering horsedrawn holidays

Right Traveller-made vans in the 1940s. They were built on existing underworks and usually shaped up according to necessity with whatever materials were to hand

cupboard for china, a locker-seat opposite the fire and a chest of drawers, the top of which serves as a table. A decorated brass or chromed bracket-lamp is attached to a swivel on the right-hand window jamb, or beside the overmantel in the Bow-top. Across the back of the waggon is the two-berthed bed-place and above it the rear window.

In the best vans there is an atmosphere of almost regal splendour with gilded carving, brilliant-cut mirrors, french-polished mahogany and ornamental brasswork. Gypsy interiors are often masterpieces of good housekeeping, resplendent with Crown Derby china, lace trimmings, and family photographs in ornate silver frames. As has already been mentioned, Gypsies are very particular about cleanliness in the home, however untidy the ground may be outside. A typical remark is: 'Living like we does you *got* to keep clean.'

The general layout of the interior had become standard by as early as 1860, evolved through experience of waggon-living over a period of years. It is doubtful if within so small a compass such high standards, aesthetic and functional, have ever been surpassed (note 9).

Top right Two doors on Wright-built waggons (*left*: Ledge; *right*: Bow top). If the customer could afford it, carving was 'flashed up', or even covered, with gold-leaf. Gypsy van doors always opened outwards, those for showmen invariably inwards. No one seems to know why. Convenience can be argued either way, but one old Traveller hinted at an explanation: 'Me and my ole gal, we's always *corin'* (fighting) ain't we!'

Bottom right Typical axle-case decoration on a Wright Ledge. Most of his vans had turned axle-cases, often with extended spring-block mountings, bridged like this one

Decoration

Above Carving, gold-leaf and paint decoration on a panelled Showman waggon built by Howcroft of West Hartlepool.

Typical porch-brackets used by Dunton on his Reading vans. The carving was contracted out with very specific requirements. On well-designed waggons it had the appearance of being a part of, and growing out of, the main structure

97

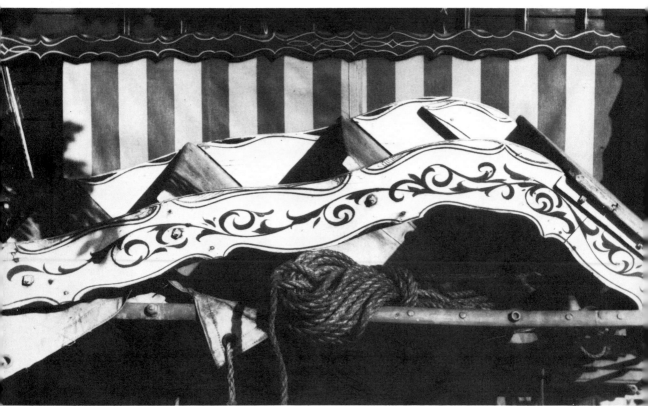

Left Carved and gilded screen over the bed-place in a Dunton Reading van. The horse-head, horseshoe and crop motif is a characteristic hallmark of Dunton-built vans

Bottom left Freehand scrolling by an experienced Gypsy painter down the side of waggon steps (loaded here on the back of a waggon). With no preliminary drawing, this is done with a 'one-stroke' sable brush as quickly as you could trace it with your finger

Right Gypsy paintwork on a contemporary Open-lot. Decoration on vans derives from Renaissance neo-classical décor which was the stock-in-trade of all decorators in the days when interior decorating was just that. The way it was put to use and the styles and motifs that eventually evolved on Gypsy vans and carts, including the elaborate 'lining-out', owes much to the Gypsies' natural liking of visual richness and ornamentation – and his love of the horse

Below One builder of Traveller stock has gained enough experience and expertise to be able to build, from the ground up, his own version of a Wright Bow-top. The photograph shows details of the forecarriage

Interiors

Above Looking forward from the bed. Behind the mirrored overmantel the chimney pipe passes through an airing cupboard with a small door above right

Left A Dunton Reading interior from the door. The wide-angle lens plays tricks with proportion; the overall interior measurement at waist height is 10 feet by 6 feet. The brilliant-cut mirrors (four) slide shut over the bed-place, and the doors beneath slide back to reveal a smaller bed where children could sleep

Facing page This is typical of what Gypsy people did with the interior of a Bow-top. When moving off to go the road, all china, silver and ornaments are stowed away in cupboards, drawers and round the mattress, cushioned with clothes and blankets. A van pulled over rough ground snaps about on its long springs like a small ship in a storm (Photos. by courtesy of P. Stretton-Ingram)

Open-lot interior. By building out over the smaller wheels of a dray, and not boxing in the fireplace, more space is achieved than in the original Bow-top van, though at the expense of exterior elegance. The bed at night can be pulled out on side rails to make a double

The Open-lot evolved slowly from the old tilted pot-carts and accommodations, and of course is still evolving. This recent design (c. 1977) dispenses with the nearside front cupboard, allowing a seat by the opening; the front panels are curved in to meet the crown-board under the porch, the step-in dip is widened, and the stanchions lathe-turned

The Trailers

The change-over from waggons to trailers did not come suddenly. (The word 'caravan' is still not used by Travellers except when talking down to the *gauji*). As far back as 1919 some forward-looking and well-to-do Travellers were having traditional van-bodies built onto motor chassis. Motor trailers as such tended to be adopted when the type of work undertaken by the individual required the use of a lorry or pick-up. Some ten years after World War II, when petrol came off the ration, many Travellers were ready for the change. The proprietary-built living-waggons were by then showing serious signs of wear. A further contributory factor was that the motor trailer was generally considered 'respectable' by landowner, citizen and police alike and was less likely to be moved on forthwith from a stopping-place beside the road. In the 1970s the pendulum has swung the other way if anything, and the well-decorated Open-lot is more likely to be tolerated for its picturesqueness and romantic connotations.

Trailers Trailers used by Travellers are not the same as those suitable for the holiday caravanner. The requirement is quite different and several caravan firms design and manufacture trailers specifically for the Travellers' market. Few Travellers for instance would tolerate the questionable *gaujo* practice of living with your Elsan. A lavatory under the same roof, let alone close to where food is prepared, is considered distasteful at best, and probably downright unhealthy.

An essential feature in most trailers is a solid fuel stove with chimney-pipe and cowl. Not uncommonly today this stove is used just for heating, a propane gas cooker being installed in the kitchen area. Unlike the holiday caravan the trailer is of course a permanent home and as

Previous page Romani carpet salesman with one of the first motorised homes, *c.*1919: the Gray family on the road with 'Nellie' and 'Drusilla'. The bobble-fringed curtains and tasselled blind are as typical today

Top On the Hill at Appleby New Fair, 1970. Typical trailer windowsill displays on the right

Above Hog's Back *atchin'-tan* before it was fenced off in 1974. The pony pulls the miniature Bow-top

Right The outside of the trailer is kept as scrupulously cleaned and polished as the interior. The attitude to the immediate surroundings outside the trailer, considered more as a working area, is also illustrated here

such is expected to have qualities that a temporary one can do without. Travellers are as house-proud as any other section of society, and to cater for this firms such as Westmorland Star of Penrith, Astral of Hull, and until recently Vickers of Morecambe, have brought out ever more resplendent travelling homes. By 1977 the Travellers' Specials reached a peak of baroque splendour and opulence, with every kind of modern comfort inside and the last available space on the outside panelled and embossed in stainless steel, coloured plastic, chrome and glitter. Chunky and elaborate chrome fender bars and overriders are mounted fore and aft and the bevel glass windows are brilliant-cut by hand with garlands, grapevines, stars and sunbursts.

In the windows, carrying on the traditions of Waggon-time, draped bobble-fringed curtains and pelmets of Belgian lace surmount tasselled roller blinds, a double bid for elegance and privacy. Serpentine glass-fronted cabinets, tables, work-tops and upholstered button-back seats are faced with simulated marble or mother-of-pearl. All remaining wall-space is lined with hand-cut mirrors, part-coloured, studded and decorated with designs like

Above These Travellers'Specials at Appleby Fair on two consecutive seasons demonstrate the steady build-up of ornamentation

Above right Two designs by Vickers c. 1976

Below right Simple Traveller baroque – a 'Safari' trailer with personalised stainless steel panels

those on the windows. These trailers for the flash Traveller can cost as much as £20,000 and the waiting list is up to nine months. It is a necessary proviso that no two trailers are identical in design.

The latest trend for Travellers' Specials is toward more restrained and clean lines – a more elegant and suave kind of appeal.

Towing Among Travellers' 'motors' the current favourites for towing and scrap are the Ford Custom Cab and the Bedford TK lorry. These will tow a heavy trailer (say 45 cwt) while avoiding the 3-ton Heavy Goods Licence. For trailers under 30 cwt, a Ford Transit twin-wheel

Range Rover and Datsun Pick-up, 1978

Below and right Three Westmorland Star trailers, also called 'West Mornin' Stars' and nicknamed 'Zebras' by Travellers. No two are identical

Above Fruit-pickers near Wisbech, 1978; an Astral 'Lavengro'. Astral's latest production, the 'Varda', is advertised as 'the product of years of experience in the special world of the Traveller and showman. With the lines of a thoroughbred, the Varda gleams like a jewel in the crown of the countryside.'

pick-up, petrol or diesel, and other Transit vans, twin or single-wheel. Some Travellers use a Datsun, Mazda or small Toyota Pick-up as a runabout and for towing a light trailer or small horse-box.

Family cars include the Range Rover, Volvo Estate and Saloon, Mercedes Benz (diesel or petrol) or the Datsun de Luxe Saloon. These are the cream for the flash Traveller; among motors as among horses and men, the élitist requirement is in no way essential to good or adequate performance. Travellers have their own pet names for motors of well-tried and tested service. 'Frog-fronted', 'Mouth-organ', and 'Showknees' are three. The last is not named after an Indian tribe, though that would be characteristic; your legs are visible through a window in the side of the cab.

Far left Flash Travellers' style, new and old. *Front to rear*: Mercedes Diesel Saloon, Vickers Trailer, Volvo Estate car, Dunton Reading waggon

Left This stall at a horse-fair caters for the trailer interior – at a price. A Crown Derby cup and saucer can cost £20 and it will not be just for show. The Capo-di-Monte groups and figurines could cost £500 or more; bought as an investment or a family heirloom

Above Luxury trailer interior, c. 1976 (Photo. Roger Perry)

Horse-fairs, High-Days and Holidays

Horse-fairs, race-meetings and crop-harvesting – these are the occasions for Gypsy gatherings, when the 'tribes' come together and exchange news; to celebrate or to mourn; when marriages are made, friendships and feuds formed, renewed or ended. All such occasions have a special air of zest and festivity and are the Travellers' equivalent of holiday-time.

Below Young Herons show a bit of style at Brough during the October fair, 1911. (*Photo. Fred Shaw*)

Right Boswells and Herons on a Sunday preparing to visit the Gypsy Gospel Mission tent for a morning service, c. 1910

Right below Epsom Races, June 1937. Due to a conflict with authority Gypsies were barred from camping in 'the Bushes' near the Racecourse. A local well-wisher, Lady Sybil Grant, provided them with a field off Downs Road to pull their waggons. Two *chavvies* are having a few rounds with 'the gloves' no doubt for a small purse – as well as to please The Times' photographer

Below Epsom Races, June 1948. The old *atchin'-tan* among the thorns; this was the last year that horsedrawn Travellers were allowed to pull on. Coopers and Brazils relax in the morning sun, the *raklies* making daisy-chains

Bottom The Hop-fields. Sunday morning at Horsmonden, 1949. The women prepare a meal for midday on two fires while menfolk hang about apparently slightly stunned after Saturday night at the *kitchema* (pub)

Bottom Horse-fair in 1978. A time to come alive; youngsters will remember with as much affection and nostalgia as their great Grandparents did

Below Boys pile on a lorry as it pauses at a road junction in town for a free ride back to the Fair Hill (Appleby, 1978)

The Horse-fair   Horse-fairs have always figured large in the Gypsies' year and in the hey-day of Waggon-time the list up and down the country was a long one. Lee Gap, Topcliffe, Boroughbridge, Appleby, Brough Hill, Brigg, Barnet, Horncastle, Bridgwater, Devizes, Stow on the Wold and many more. Some of these date back 800 years or further. They would draw Travellers and drovers from all over the country. Gypsies, unfamiliar with calendar dates, would converge with their cavalcades and small convoys of waggons during the previous weeks and camp within easy distance to be ready for the day. At Appleby today the Travellers start 'pulling on' a week before the fair and eventually form a Gypsy city crowning the hill behind the town. There they come into their own, like the Jews returning to Israel for one week only. Everyone enjoys it including the police save for the odd incident; the good-natured banter between the Gypsy and the Law is something to see.

The number of horse-fairs has steadily diminished, but those like Appleby and Stow still draw Travellers from all over the British Isles and even across the world. Hundreds of horses change hands at prices that can range from fifty to several thousand pounds. Trading is also in trailers, waggons, flat-carts, harness, clothing, footwear, bedding, cushions, china, glass and jewellery – all the gear and trappings of Traveller culture.

The road to Brough and Kirkby Stephen. 'I'm a Rovin' Jack ...' is a song still sung in pubs frequented by Travelling people. One of the fifty-odd verses runs:

'Now there's a horse I bought and sold,
A stallion, colt or brood-mare;
I bought them in the winter's time
And sold them at the horse-fair.
At Barnet and at Appleby
They know me well in season,
You'll always find me at Brough Hill
Likewise in Kirkby Stephen.'

Shouts clear the way through the crowd and bareback riders wheel and turn as a flat-cart goes by at a bone-shaking trot. Though there is much hard riding you never see a saddle at a Travellers' horse-fair

Outside the Hare and Hounds. This is the main street in Appleby at opening-time. Horses line the curb and fill the pub yard. Many of them have been brought down from the Hill for a morning wash in the River Eden by the bridge. Some of the pubs close during fair-week; the ones that stay open, and the shops, do prodigious trade

119

Breakfast visiting at the Fair. Old-timers like the blind Gypsy poet (note 10) would not miss Appleby-time in June

A camp haircut from grandfather Sylvester Gordon Boswell (Photo. Richard Wade)

Washing the Horses

Washing the horses in the River Eden is a morning ritual above the bridge at Appleby during fair week. Boys and girls often inadvertently get a wash at the same time (note 11)

The Gypsy Sport

The Appleby Trot – trotting races held in the evening on a course laid out in a meadow behind the town – provides an opportunity during fair week to show off magnificent horses and first-rate horsemanship (Photo. Richard Wade)

Bottom Selling a trotter

Early morning departure the day after the fair. A waggon and flat-cart like this could have changed hands several times over the past week

Right Suitable open spaces for Travellers to test and demonstrate the speed and stamina of their horses are getting few and far between. This newspaper cutting records a classic example of Gypsy spirit and initiative. Date: 1978

Gypsies seal off part of A1 for dawn horse race

Police in Nottinghamshire are looking into complaints that gypsies shut off seven miles of the Great North Road with their vehicles and turned it into a racecourse.

Villagers alongside the A1 between Sutton-on-Trent and Tuxford said yesterday that 250 gypsies, some from as far away as Scotland, closed the road for 20 minutes while two gypsy families decided which of them owned the best horse. One family was from Surrey and one from Doncaster. Each staked £2,000 on the race along the A1. Side bets totalled several thousand pounds.

The race, run at 6 am, on Sunday last week, was won by the northern horse, which completed the course in 19 minutes. After the race the winning owner rejected an offer of £3,500 for it.

Police in the town of Retford, near by, said: "We did not know it was happening and we are looking into it No one has the right to close a trunk road, certainly not for horse racing." But inquiries were difficult because the gypsies left the district after the race.

Marriage was always considered a personal affair and though bureaucratic requirements today dictate a church or registry office wedding it used to be very much a tribal matter, the joining of hands and affirmation to each other before witnesses being wholly binding. When a couple agreed to wed it was customary to 'run away' together, reappearing a week or so later for the marriage rites. Courtship is restrained; any physical intimacy before the decision to marry was, and still is, unusual and frowned on. Concerning marital fidelity, the record is high and though domestic rows are far from uncommon, desertion, separation or divorce are rare.

Left Wedding at a village church in Surrey, 1947

Above Hearns, Burtons, Smiths, Lees and Ryles at a wedding near Pontypridd in the twenties

Below A wedding feast near Swansea, 1966

Music Gypsies in Britain, as in other countries, have adopted and to some degree helped to keep alive local country music and dance. The ancient and intricate step-dance, performed individually like an Irish jig, can often still be seen in those pubs and other places where Travellers celebrate – in the open performed on a board thrown down for the purpose. Some very old folksongs have been retained and remain current among travelling people, and a small but highly characteristic selection of popular songs are gathered up and added to the repertoire along the way.

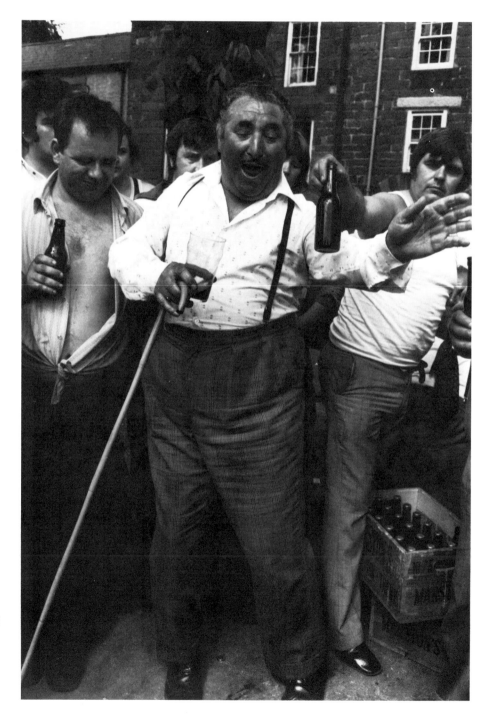

The Sands, Appleby, 1976. Crowded out of the pub, Travellers cross the road and have a song on the banks of the river Eden. The long cane is almost a symbol of office of the North Country horse-dealer. (Photo. J. K./Magnum)

A couple of Gypsy *boshomengros* (fiddlers) and a harpist entertain on the sands at Barmouth, N. Wales, c.1905. *Left to right*: Cornelius, Llewellyn and Davey Wood. The fiddles are home-made by the Woods from reinforced cedarwood cigar-boxes – a practice by no means to be despised since the wood, and the proportion, provided resonance and depth of tone

Below left Another Welsh Gypsy musician – Matthew Wood at Bangor, 1914

Fiddle-player in Dorset, 1977, accompanied by his son, who would rather play a guitar! The fiddler tradition goes on but the most popular instrument by far is the piano accordion

The popular image of guitar-playing Gypsies is an import from Europe. These Gypsies reached Barnet via Belgium in 1921. The waggon is English (Photo. Fred Shaw)

Hanging to dry from a twist of barbed wire under the back porch of a waggon: Horehound (for colds, coughs and constipation), Tansy (for kidney and liver troubles) and something else which defies classification

Medicine   There has always been an extensive inherited knowledge of the properties of wild plants among Gypsies, although this appears to be much on the decline. It was common in the old days to see little bunches of dried herbs hanging in the van or under the waggon-porch. Today the Traveller when hard-pressed leans more heavily on doctor and hospital though the *puri dai* (old mother), with her infusions and salves, is still to be found. Like so much inherited knowledge the practitioners know that it works though they may not know how. For instance, there is evidence that Gypsies have long known the properties of penicillin. A family in Kent, for as long as any remember, have kept a pot of jam at hand growing mould for the treatment of open wounds. They find its antiseptic and healing qualities are spectacular and without equal.

Funeral Rites   One of the best-known Gypsy customs, even now adhered to in rare instances, is the ritual burning of the van and destruction of the possessions of the dead. This undoubtedly has its roots far back in time but it seems likely that it has survived in 20th century England mainly through a combination of Romany fastidiousness and a superstitious fear of the *mullo* (ghost), reinforced in the case of waggon-burning by the old Gypsy view that there is something basically unhealthy about four walls and a roof anyway.

The burning of Luke Smith's waggon in the field where he stopped near Beverton, Gloucestershire, 1947

Top Cottage tent used for a Gypsy funeral on the Welsh borders in the 1940s

Above June 1978; the fresh grave of a 19-year-old Traveller on Epsom Downs in the cemetery near the racecourse. Floral tributes, some in the form of lorry-and-trailer, Transit van, hearts, horseshoes, and overflowing beer-mugs, lined the walk for fifty yards each side of the grave

'Foreign' Gypsies in England

Bottom left Macedonian Gypsies at Royston pose for the photographer with the local constabulary, *c.* 1905

Before 1914, and to a lesser extent between the Wars, large families of Gypsies on the move from across Europe took ship to England with their tents and waggons – some just to visit and return, a few to stay, most en route for America. Many hundreds of thousands who remained in Europe were to suffer the same fate as the Jews at the hands of the Nazis.

Transylvanian coppersmith Gypsies at Birkenhead
in 1912. A group very similar was seen at Epsom
Races in 1949

Anti-nomadic Measures

From the 1930s onwards, open heath and commonland that had been resorted to by Travellers for hundreds of years became increasingly barred to them. When they did stop there, as they sometimes had to do, they found themselves subject to savage fines. This became the Gypsies' equivalent to paying rates – but without any civic advantages. Since 1950, on many of the old stops, notices like that shown below have been superseded by fences, banks and ditches, effectively sealing off the open land. By the mid-1960s there was growing pressure from local authorities and Residents' Associations for Parliament to pass some form of repressive legislation against the Traveller. This culminated in the passing of the 1968 Caravan Sites Act, an Act which was presented as a pro-Gypsy measure but which contained a number of clauses that have subsequently backfired on the Traveller. When a Council had

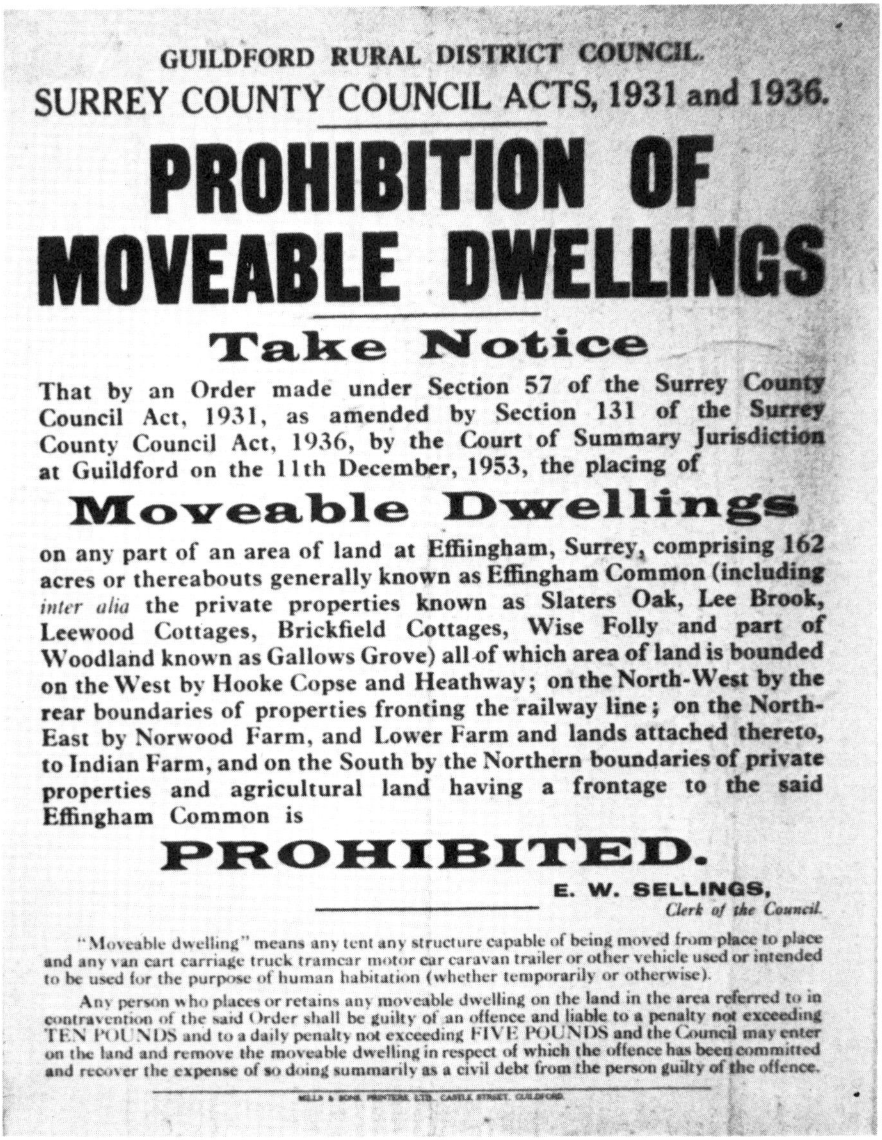

GUILDFORD RURAL DISTRICT COUNCIL.

SURREY COUNTY COUNCIL ACTS, 1931 and 1936.

PROHIBITION OF MOVEABLE DWELLINGS

Take Notice

That by an Order made under Section 57 of the Surrey County Council Act, 1931, as amended by Section 131 of the Surrey County Council Act, 1936, by the Court of Summary Jurisdiction at Guildford on the 11th December, 1953, the placing of

Moveable Dwellings

on any part of an area of land at Effiingham, Surrey, comprising 162 acres or thereabouts generally known as Effingham Common (including *inter alia* the private properties known as Slaters Oak, Lee Brook, Leewood Cottages, Brickfield Cottages, Wise Folly and part of Woodland known as Gallows Grove) all of which area of land is bounded on the West by Hooke Copse and Heathway; on the North-West by the rear boundaries of properties fronting the railway line; on the North-East by Norwood Farm, and Lower Farm and lands attached thereto, to Indian Farm, and on the South by the Northern boundaries of private properties and agricultural land having a frontage to the said Effingham Common is

PROHIBITED.

E. W. SELLINGS,
Clerk of the Council.

"Moveable dwelling" means any tent any structure capable of being moved from place to place and any van cart carriage truck tramcar motor car caravan trailer or other vehicle used or intended to be used for the purpose of human habitation (whether temporarily or otherwise).

Any person who places or retains any moveable dwelling on the land in the area referred to in contravention of the said Order shall be guilty of an offence and liable to a penalty not exceeding TEN POUNDS and to a daily penalty not exceeding FIVE POUNDS and the Council may enter on the land and remove the moveable dwelling in respect of which the offence has been committed and recover the expense of so doing summarily as a civil debt from the person guilty of the offence.

MILLS & SONS, PRINTERS, LTD. CASTLE STREET, GUILDFORD.

Effingham Common, 1950

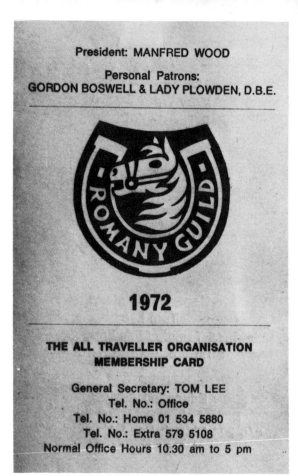

President: MANFRED WOOD

Personal Patrons:
GORDON BOSWELL & LADY PLOWDEN, D.B.E.

ROMANY GUILD

1972

THE ALL TRAVELLER ORGANISATION
MEMBERSHIP CARD

General Secretary: TOM LEE
Tel. No.: Office
Tel. No.: Home 01 534 5880
Tel. No.: Extra 579 5108
Normal Office Hours 10.30 am to 5 pm

Above Mitcham Common, 1960

Below Milton Heath, 1974

Right Romany Guild Membership Card

provided the minimum requirement under the Act, it could apply for, and usually received, a Designation Order which meant that any Travellers not on the official site were outlawed from the area that in many cases had been their home ground for generations.

The period when this Act was being conceived coincided with the emergence of pressure groups initiated by *gaujies* boldly claiming to speak for the whole Traveller community. It is difficult at this juncture to assess the long-term effect of their intervention. By 1972 some Gypsies had acquired enough insight into *gaujo* politics and Local Government motives to see the need to found their own all-Traveller organisation, the Romany Guild (inspired by the long-established Showman's Guild). Travellers felt the cause was really achieving recognition when the Guild Secretary and his wife were guests at the Queen's Garden Party at Buckingham Palace. The Romany Guild's Reports on the Caravan Sites Act are required reading and of great potential help to Councils responsible for its implementation (note 12).

Many Councils, having closed off the old pitches, were still, nearly ten years after the

Bank and ditch at a stopping-place, 1970

Act was passed, side-stepping their minimum obligation under the Act to provide sites. Housedwellers' fears of loss of amenity, and other objections sometimes bordering on hysterical fantasy, caused even the meanest proposed site to be turned down. On the other hand, as is pointed out in a recent Guild report, some Councils have provided 'vastly expensive and over-equipped miniature residential caravan sites while ignoring some of the basic requirements of the Travellers. What Travellers want and need are (transit) sites with (1) Open space large enough for living, parking and working; (2) Water; (3) Rubbish skips; (4) Elsan disposal facilities. Expensive facilities like hard-standing, electricity, flush toilets, etc Travellers are quite prepared to do without ...' As so often happens, the 'Gypsy Problem' seems to be very largely what the housedweller and bureaucrat wish to make it.

Above Hog's Back barricade, 1974

Above right These Gypsies were lucky to find such a delightful roadside stop as this one near Pembury, Kent, in September 1978

Right Three weeks later when I passed the place again the Gypsies had been moved on and a fence and ditch had already been made to prevent any further stopping. (It was only when the picture was printed that the symbolic significance of the shadow became apparent, calling to mind the Gypsy legend of the Fourth Nail (note 13)).

138

'Society has always found the Romanies an ethnic puzzle and has tried ceaselessly to fit them, by force or fraud, piety or policy, coaxing or cruelty, into some framework of its own conception, but so far without success . . .'

Stuart Mann (Encyclopaedia Britannica)

'We's the last only remaining Grasshoppers left in a world of Ants.'

English Gypsy Saying

Notes

1 Didikai: this is the spelling adopted by early Gypsiologists. The 'kai' being guttural has led to the popular alternative spelling, didicoi.

2 For a brilliantly clear, sympathetic and highly readable analysis of the English Traveller see *Gypsies and Government Policy in England* by Barbara Adams, Judith Oakley, David Morgan and David Smith. Heinemann, 1975.

3 *The Book of Boswell, the Autobiography of a Gypsy* by Sylvester Gordon Boswell, edited by John Seymour. Gollancz, 1972. A most important book.

4 For detailed information of early 20th century Gypsy dress I have leaned heavily on two articles in the Journal of the Gypsy Lore Society written by An Old Member (F. G. Huth) and illustrated with drawings by Beshlie; Vol. XXVIII Parts 1–2, and Vol. XXXIX Parts 1–2, in the Third Series (1959–60).

5 Reproduced from *Romany Life* by Frank Cuttriss. Mills and Boon Ltd, 1915.

6 From *Reminiscences of Life on the Roads* by Brian Raywid; Journal of the Gypsy Lore Society, Vol. XLVII Parts 3–4 (1968).

7 *Smoke in the Lanes* by Dominic Reeve, illustrated by Beshlie. Constable and Co Ltd, 1958; a classic evocation of the last of Waggon-time.·

8 *My Gypsy Days – Recollections of a Romani Rawnie*, by Dora E. Yates. Phoenix House Ltd, 1953.

9 For further reading see *The English Gypsy Caravan*, by C. H. Ward-Jackson and Denis E. Harvey (illustrated by Harvey). David & Charles Ltd, 1972, '72, '78; the standard work on the subject.

10 Edwin 'Lavengro' Smith. A book of his poems and ballads, *The Gypsy* (Midas Books, 1973), profusely illustrated by Juliet Jeffery, strongly evokes the English Gypsy scene.

11 For more on this theme see *A Time to Come Alive* by Wilfred Hall Associates, Harrogate, Yorkshire; a unique photographic evocation of Appleby horse-fair.

12 *The Caravan Sites Act – Eight Years On*, Romany Guild Report, 1976. The Romany Guild Office, 9 Tavistock Place, London W.C.1.

13 There are many variants of the Gypsy crucifixion legend. As I first heard it told, by Surrey Coopers in 1949, it was like this: A Gypsy stopping in Jerusalem, being a stranger in that region, was ordered to forge four nails for the cross of Christ. It was only after he had made three nails and was hammering out the fourth that he overheard what the nails were to be used for. The Gypsy, who had been hearing rumours about the Son of God, flung away the half-forged nail and fled. Ever-afterwards the Gypsies have kept on the move, hounded by the nail that reappears, glowing red-hot, if ever they should settle down.

Further recommended reading is Beshlie's *Here Today, Gone Tomorrow*. Broomsleigh Press, 1978. A potent distillation from the grass-roots of the Travellers' world.

Acknowledgments

I want to thank Brian Raywid for his patience and thoroughness in going through the manuscript for me and offering welcome encouragement, timely criticism, and some valuable suggestions including advice on the history and context of the Caravan Sites Act. My thanks are also due to the Librarian of Liverpool University for permission to use early Gypsy photographs from the Scott-Macfie Collection and particularly to Michael Perkin, the Curator of Special Collections at the University, for his help in the search for specific pictures and for allowing me to print from old negatives. I also thank Fred Huth for his generosity on lending me many pictures given to him by his old friend Fred Shaw (1867–1950) whose unique series of Gypsy photographs now forms part of the Scott-Macfie Collection.

Those who have also been of help include Tony Boxall, Graham Bishop, Julian Brotherton, Tom Clarke, A. Hippisley-Coxe, Ian Cruickshank, Tony Drewett, Daniel Harvey, Beshlie Heron. Peter Ingram, Juliet Jeffery, Josef Koudelka, Jevan Lipscomb, Mervyn Jones, Tony Lewery, Seni and Mary Matthews, John Pickett, John A. Pockett, Ron Rayner, George Reeve, Henry and Jean Smith, Richard Wade, Fred and Bella Walker, Mike Wall, C. H. Ward-Jackson, Michael and Ann Wilson, Dick and Barbara Worrall and others.

My particular thanks are due to my wife Rita for her forbearance and help over a long period.

Finally I must acknowledge my own responsibility for the short-comings and omissions in this account of the Travellers' way of life. This book is the work of an amateur in the literary field without much of a penchant for academic or sociological research; its justification is outlined in the Preface. It is largely a spin-off from experience gained over thirty-odd years on the periphery of the Travellers' world with no thought of a book in mind – the result of observation and participation rather than inquiry. As such it suffers in places from being confined to a personal viewpoint in time and space.

D.E.H.
Dorking, December 1978

Index

144